THE CASTLES WE BUILD ON LOVE & RUIN

POETRY

SASHA-LEE FINDLAY

ISBN: 978-0-620-88060-2

Putty Perfect Publishing. www.puttyperfect.co.za

CONTENTS

For anyone who has loved or been loved.
For those who are in love and those who stand on the outskirts.

For my parents, my fiancé, my circle.

To you, my reader, I hope you are stirred.

PART 1

THE VOW

Like the flower to the sun

I will open my heart to you for love

like the seas obey the moon

so too I will let you lead me

and just as the soil is to the dwellers

you are my provider

this I vow

for one is lost without the other

till mother nature calls back what was always hers

till dust returns to dust.

SOUL'S INK

I spill my soul out onto these pages

with ink I expose to you

my innermost

and you read me with such

indulgence

savoring each word

each letter

each fragment of my essence

treating my delicate pages

with the caution of a first time driver

a story yet to be completed

though still wanting

to you I will always be

an open book.

CRUSH

Pardon me I do believe

that you've just looked my way

and if I'm not mistaken

I hear what your eyes do say

they brighten when I am near and quiver when we speak

could it possibly be that you feel something for me

though I'm quite unsure where this would lead

I do know one thing

you've already planted the seed

your eyes they seem to me so wanting yet so meek

what exactly is it from me that you seek

say the words and I shall reply

courage young man give it a try

for I am much weaker than I may seem

what my eyes do beg

please do deem.

HOMELY GIRL

She never seemed to like anything fun
like going on rides at the fair
or going to the movies
taking strolls in the park
or partying after dark
instead she'd sit on her porch swing
humming and wondering
why the moon only shines when kissed by the sun
and I'd walk past her house
whistling and thinking
that someday she'd be the one.

LUNAR LOVE

I will love you like the moon loves the earth

for the moon understands no other gravity

than that of the earth

and in turn

mother earth leaves her seas

unto the mercy

of her lunar deity.

—

"He makes all the right moves

as if we've danced to this love before."

EVE

He became so aroused

when he traced a path down the arch of her back

when he outlined the organic curves of her hips butt and thighs

when he stroked her dainty legs down and up

when he walked his fingers up her ribcage

and when he cupped her soft breasts

he found pleasure in all that she was

that he was not.

MY LOVER

My lover loves like a summer rain

his strong downpour gives life to my soil

as I blossom for him

my lover loves like a summer sun

his darting rays kissing my tanned skin

blissfully basking in his presence

I beg him to stay

just one more day

for there is no love more forgiving

than that of my lover.

FEELS

He made her feel

consciously feel

from the tips of her fingers

to the tips of her toes

her head rushed

her cheeks blushed

he made her feel

more than she'd like to reveal.

EDEN

She was the beginning and end of him. Intricately woven, he needed to know every inch that was her.

Unknown territory. She was like the garden of Eden

A stroll through her voluptuous valley, the rise and fall of her tumulus hills brought him to a sweat quicker than an instant.

A dip in her cavernous cove echoed his name against soft rock of the surrounding walls, he ventured through her lush forests until he stumbled upon her cave where he entered, touching each wall with pleasure, holidaying in the remnants of visitors past, leaving his own trace for explorers to come.

Together, he experienced heaven in a moment, for he was discovering Eden and he found it blissfully absorbing.

—

"You touch my body

like you've read my fantasies in a book."

HOT

His trembling voice whispers in her ear

as his hot breath caresses her damp skin

her fingertips gently work their way up the centre of his chest

outlining each little imperfection along the way

if it's not madly passionate

it's not a lifetime.

AUTUMN GIRL

She was never a winter wonderland

shades of grey and building snowmen were never her

she was never a spring fling

bright colours and blossoming buds were never her

she was never a summer splash

soft pastels and cocktails on the beach were never her

she was an autumn girl

her warmth was intoxicating

reds browns and yellows

her mystery was hypnotising

and if you took the time you'd see that though her leaves had fallen

and icy times approach

she had space in her heart for new life and new love.

LOVER

But she's only eighteen you say

how could he fall so hard for her

how could he love her so defiantly

how could a man so mature grow so naive

but he was a man

lost in love in love

with her blonde hair blue eyes

yet in her presence

he was but a boy in love with a girl.

SOULMATES

Whoever said soulmates are a myth is clearly mistaken because tonight I gave you a little bit of my soul

in exchange for a little bit of yours.

"I love you more than there are stars

unconditionally

through all our lives

that is all."

DAYS

Some days

I want to dance with you beneath the stars

and some days

I want to dwell with you beneath your scars.

PARALLEL PATHS

Sometimes it feels like

we're travelling in the same direction

yet on parallel paths

and I just don't know if

we'll ever merge at the end of it all.

"The stars in your eyes light up the endless black hole

in which my love dwells."

PART 2

BROWN EYES

He made her cry so often
she wore the look with pride
the red really brought out
the colour in her eyes.

NOON

He left before noon
he left me in swoon
sneaking out like a stolen full moon
he left before noon.

"A thousand secrets lay neatly laced into my soul

waiting till the night is gone

wanting to be confessed."

THIEF

Ain't it funny

how you just walked in my life

and shut the door to everyone else

how you claimed all my joy and zest

and handed me your tattered loneliness

how my windows to the world are covered

in layers and layers of dust

while yours shimmer with a smug sparkle

how I'm sitting here in a dark dingy corner

bruised and battered

from the top to the bottom of my weakened heart

thinking how funny it is that the day I died

you came alive.

MÄDCHEN IN DER NACHT

She was the maiden of the night

clothed in a silky gown of moonlight

she roamed the streets in plain sight

every lost and drunken soul swooned by her presence

her touch a deathly decadence

it was said that she lured them with her sweet song

the sound of a mockingjay

and if you hummed along to her entrancing song

she'd wrap you in her flowing gown

and to the shadows you'd both return

the moon and the stars be my witness

many a men had been lost to her darkness.

JUST LIKE THAT

You left in the dead of night

now all my yesterdays and tomorrows

are made of happy memories

and floods of sorrow.

PIECES

A silver smile

that turns my knees to jelly

a real gentleman worthy of a crown

then when the sunset fades

and the strong wind glides through the trees a fever I can't bear

like chains restraining my soul

when I finally rise up you break me down

an eternal fear I have for you

when I fall to pieces

because of you.

WAX

Just like a candle

you bring light to my life

but just like a candle

you also bring pain

as my house burns to the ground

your flames touch me

your wax seeps into my skin

you've left your mark on my soul

as my blood marks the ashen walls.

MEMORY

She awoke in the dead of the night and followed footprints outside to where the stars stain the sky.

The icy midnight air kissing the nape of her neck, the moon begs her leave this place, the stars beg her to pick up the pace, but her legs won't move.

She's afraid to let go, afraid to move away from his black love.

The echo of her heartbeat reminds her of the great rhythm of love they once danced to, she blinks to the rhythm of a distant clock ticking, wishing the world would rewind every time she opens her eyes.

Oh sweet memory, that is all it will only be, a ghost of a moment that was and she would always wish it back.

But now she must think only of herself and run!

Memories are horrible friends but it is all she has left.

The breeze sweeps her up and she lets herself be carried away to a place of quietened fears.

I

"For it is not the skeletons in our closets

that would haunt us

but our shallow graves we mount for all to see."

REFLECTION

She was a living, breathing body of life

so how was she supposed to compete with an image

she asked herself

how were her imperfect curves going to match

the perfectly carved figure

just sitting there

on the bright screen

how could he say she was perfect for him

when perfection stared her in the face

and she knew how far from it she was.

TEARS IN THE DARK

She used to be a perfect picture of a thousand sunsets

but he had painted her in black and white

she used to be so alive

but his shadow cast a veil of death over her

stunted growth

she had nowhere to go

a trapped soul

he had done her foul

her love had always been stark

but lately she's been crying all her tears in the dark.

I

"Sweet words herald bitter fists."

STILL

I still get the nightmares

I still feel your hands wrapped around my heart

strangling

choking

till the very last

wisp of love had left my chest

and I still wake up and turn to my new love

wondering if one day maybe

he'll turn out to be just like you

because once upon a time

you started out just like him.

|

"Take what you must from me

but all I ask is that you leave my sanity."

SLAVE

Oh

caress my soul

tenderly

your sharp tongue embraces

sweet words

foolishly my soul believes

blind to your mockery

have your way with me dear lie for I am yours

to have and to enfold.

ENVY

She'll come like a thief in the night

harvesting all your dreams to fulfil her own

she'll consume your being, your mind

suck your soul dry, void of all happiness

you won't know she's alive

a malignant tumor

till she has devoured every inch of you

your joy / your psyche / your self

with the grit of an army

she won't stop until you disintegrate into the abyss

one day you'll wake up

and she will be your new soul

you'll look into the mirror

see her looking back

and call yourself Envy.

"She fixed him a sandwich and a drink

with a sprinkle of love

and a dash of arsenic."

QUICKSAND

We've been here before

and you've crushed my soul before

but now I've guarded my fragile core

kept your menacing enchantment at bay

yet you come again

returning to the site of destruction

and my soul, she knows you

your familiar smell and familiar words, and she succumbs

so I try to run

faster than the crumbling walls of my heart

faster than the stream flowing from my eyes

moving faster and faster...

if only

my centre wasn't cemented in you.

—

"Doomed to dwell in mania

my fixation erodes my core."

RESIDUE

Your kisses taste like darkness

with a hint of death

your black travels from the top of my tongue

to the ends of my veins

your demons feed off my spirit

you cannot expect colourful rainbows drawn for you

by this charcoal heart

but I assure you, it's sinister portraits are beautiful just the same

there is life in this decay.

DEATH BECKONS ME

I woke up one night

without a single breath

I saw my soul take flight

I must have met Death

he said he came to fetch me

but I begged to stay

come now he coaxed me

I've fetched plenty more today

but in an instant all had vanished, had Death now taken flight?

I opened my eyes to the one whom I cherished

and knew why I hardly had to put up a fight

he saw your light in my heart

now my soul and I are no longer apart.

CURTAIN CALL

It's time for the curtain call

we could've had it all

but this is the leap before the fall

so let's leave the stage and stop the performance

our love was all the rage but in my life it's created a disturbance

I'll leave you to your encore

as the crowd pleads for more and more

I'll take the humble second place

and relax my bones as I forget your face.

PAPER CUT

Like a paper cut

you are insignificant to the body

but painful to the mind

I don't see you

but you've left a burning in my heart.

SHADOWS

There is darkness in us all

no matter how small

and it haunts us

even in the light.

—

He asked her why she cried so much
"It's all my eyes have known."

IN MY HEART

My heart

heavy laden

with pains of past and burdens of future

the watermark of

words left unsaid

deeds left for dead

stained with the dying love

of the one who comes and goes

like the wind

the raindrops on my head

are invisible

in the dark

like the sorrow in my heart.

|

"Ah

her love is such sweet sorrow

like a daisy blossoming upon a grave."

REMORSE

When you try to love, you think of pain

when you feel pain, you think of me

I'm nothing but an obstacle

I see you struggle to get over me

and maybe I'm sorry.

BLANKET OF LOVE

Bring your heart

and come snuggle in my blanket of love

leave your insecurities at the door

for the fire of my affection only burns with

flames of passion and adoration

leave a crack in the window

the world's cold air will only let you snuggle deeper

under my blanket of love.

MOTH

Like a moth to a flame

I've never had a love so hot

and these burn scars

are the only reminder of a love once alight

the only piece of you still haunting me.

—

"You are a lie I tell myself

just to get by

just to keep my soul alive."

LOVE ME

She makes it look so easy to love you

I wish I was her

and you were you

then maybe you could love me too.

—

"So I draw the blinds and shut the door
if I don't see the world
maybe they'll forget I exist."

PART 3

SUMMER

This lonely winter morning
made my aching heart realise
that summer lies
in your big brown eyes.

"Maybe it's the way you so casually walk

that I'm still left confused

if you're walking with me

or away from me."

REGARDS

I'll send my regards to your new girl

and let her know how you rocked my world

all we have left are memories

ghosts of everything we were

fallen leaves of good times had

cuts and scars

our passion was had

so my tears they fall no more

I'll send my hellos to your new girl

and let her know that I've shut that door.

—

"I'll help you love me better

all you have to do is stay awhile

my desires are echoed through my smile."

LAST DANCE

Their love was a dance ever so passionate

he'd toss her up

spin her around

and catch her before she hit the ground

but one day he let her fall

and that is all.

CROSSROADS

They stood at the sign love or infatuation and they chose the shorter
of the two roads. Hand in hand fingers intertwined they happily
skipped along and the road ended abruptly. It ended as quickly as it
started and they went their separate paths thereafter

satisfied.

MAYBE

Maybe I lie a little more

maybe I cry a little more

maybe I laugh a little more

maybe I talk a little more

maybe I dance a little more

maybe I show a little more

maybe I love you a little more

and maybe I hope you feel a little more.

—

"He spent his days searching

for the light in her eyes

but the sun had already set in her heart."

GASP

I've dwelled in the depths of your love

suffocated by the beauty of the deep

I've swum to the surface and I realised I can breathe

the beach isn't as pretty as the deep blue sea

but at least I can breathe.

"Sometimes love alone is not enough

and sometimes it is too much."

A THOUSAND SUNS

Remember when you took my heart

you also took my youth

my beauty

my dreams

and when you left me out in the dark

it was as though my heart had been dragged

through the fires of a thousand suns

the charred remains of a genuine love

not even the hands of the gods could revive.

BYE

I watched her say goodbye to him
and though she felt like winter frost
her tears to me were a summer rain
washing away the old and dead
bringing forth new life again.

WHEN SHE WAS

His broken bones

remind him that his past was real

sometimes he forgets

that he didn't just wake up one day

hollow and unable to feel

sometimes he forgets of the joy he once felt

a feeling perplexing to him now

her radiant sentences fill his mind

and his eyes begin to kindle

he feels the warmth of words thanks to her

her smile had illuminated his being

and he loved dancing

in her contagious ambience.

|

"He was just a little bit weaker

and she was just a little bit stronger

and it seeped through the cracks when they separated

every time."

LOVED

She loved ruthlessly

and she swore to love him entirely

so that he may never wake any day

feeling alone and unloved

for he would know that there was at least one person in this world

that loved him

when not even he loved himself.

"She reads a book

gazing across the street

waiting for someone that she'll never meet."

HER SELF

She lay there feeling her breasts
they've sagged a little over the years
so has her butt
and her thighs
and her stomach
everything has wilted
along with her happiness.

—

"Of all the things
he made her feel
nothing more
and nothing less."

SIGH

But when she came home

she was alone

the quiet suffocated her

as she sat by the kitchen counter listening to

the house breathe

the doors creek

the floors groan

as they breathe a sigh of relief

it is no consolation that her wilted spirit

her melancholy and gloom

were the fruits that fed this

home.

MERMAID

Loving you was like diving into the ocean
and finding a beautiful underwater cave
you were everything pretty
and everything deep.

BETWEEN

I tried to put my heart back together

but I just couldn't succeed

until I realised that

I still had pieces of you

in between pieces of me.

For Tashie

Your life was short lived but my memories of you know no end. I hear your laugh, I see your smile, I smell your sweet innocence and feel your warmth.

I carry you in my pen and in my heart.

BUTTERFLY

And when the angels come to fetch you

they unchain your shackled soul

you are free from the weight of this world

oh, crushed and fragile spirit

and so you float up

higher and freer

like the butterfly you always were

towards the paradise you most deserve.

FOREST CALLING

The fairies are here

they've come to take me home

the pixies are chanting my name

worry not my love

for I leave you one last kiss

one last dream

so that you may roam in my wonderland

till the forest beckons you too.

ABOUT THE AUTHOR

Sasha-Lee Findlay is a young writer from Johannesburg, South Africa. She has pursued a life in creation and busies herself with arts and crafts, design and writing in all her free moments.

"Writing has always been a part of my life. I create for the world, even if it's just one person's world."

Sasha-Lee owns a small self publishing company and enjoys using her expertise and experience in design and writing to help authors around the world realise their dreams of being self published and see their works and visions come to life.